To: _____

From: _____

Other books by Gregory E. Lang:

Why a Daughter Needs a Dad

Why a Son Needs a Dad

Why I Love Grandma

Why I Love Grandpa

Why a Son Needs a Mom

Why a Daughter Needs a Mom

Why I Chose You

Why I Love You

Why I Need You

Why We Are a Family

Brothers and Sisters

Love Signs

Life Maps

Simple Acts

WHY WE ARE FRIENDS

100 reasons

GREGORY E. LANG

CUMBERLAND HOUSE

NASHVILLE, TENNESSEE

WHY WE ARE FRIENDS
PUBLISHED BY CUMBERLAND HOUSE PUBLISHING, INC.
431 Harding Industrial Drive
Nashville, TN 37211

ISBN-13: 1-978-58182-555-8
ISBN-10: 1-58182-555-2

Cover design: Unlikely Suburban Design
Text design: Lisa Taylor
Photographs and cover photo: Gregory E. Lang

Printed in the United States of America
1 2 3 4 5 6 7 8 9 10 — 11 10 09 08 07 06

To Jill—the best friend of my life.

Introduction

I have been blessed with many friends in my life. Some I've met at school, work, church, or in the neighborhood. Others I've met at unexpected places, as when waiting in line at an airport, sitting on a porch while on vacation, or even in the course of writing my books, as I've approached complete strangers to ask if I could take their photograph.

Some friends are the kind of people you are happy to spend time with, with whom you exchange pleasantries and share stories and events of your life, but who have a place in your life only for a particular period in time. This period may be long or short, marked by fun and laughter or common pain and struggle, yet it proved to be the bond on which the friendship grew. These times are meaningful, memorable for the special circumstances that emerged and created a new friendship. Even though your lives may have taken different paths, this person, this friend, remains a lasting memory in your heart and mind.

Other friends are the kind you share a relationship with that spans time, the kind of friend you may not have seen in years but who will give you a warm hug upon seeing you again and then keep you awake for hours "catching up." These are the friends with whom you never need to warm up to, the ones that you know you can count on and who know they can count on you. These friends are the kind you can sit on a porch with and never say a word and yet feel completely at ease. These are the friends with whom you are vulnerable because they know so much about you but with whom you are safe because they love you as much as you love them.

And then there are those friends who rise to the status of best friend, the friend who is irreplaceable, the friend you think about often, who you miss when you are apart, for whom you will do practically anything, if not everything. These are the friends who always walk alongside you, who pull or push you as needed, who care for your heart and soul, who never turn their back on you, ignore your need for help, or fail to take your phone call.

What makes someone a best friend varies, I think, for each of us. For some a best friend can only be a same-sex companion, but for others a best friend could be either gender or any age. Some claim a sibling, a spouse, or even a parent as their best friend. What is so unique about the best-friend relationship is that there are no criteria for it; it is simply a matter of personal choice, whether that choice is obvious or not. No two best friends are just like any other two. In fact, there may be nothing in common about best friends, but no matter, because no one you claim as your best friend can be proven otherwise.

I have had a few best friends—my cousin with whom I spent most of my free time as a teenager, a cheerleader in high school who to this day tells me she loves me even though we may not have seen each other in years, a fellow I met in college and then stayed in touch with for years and through many difficult times for both of us, and others still. Today my best friend is my wife, Jill, and she will be my best friend for the rest of my life. She and my memories of those who now hold or have held important places in my life are the inspiration for this book. There are times when I want to call each of these people and tell them of my gratitude for having them in my life, to thank them for being my friend. I am who I am because all of them in their own way have given something of themselves to me, and having done so, left an indelible imprint on me. They changed me.

On second thought, perhaps there is something all best friends have in common. They always give something of themselves to each other, and both are the better for it. As you read this book, I hope you recognize something of what your best friend has given you.

WHY WE ARE FRIENDS

We Are Friends Because

we grow closer and closer, day by day.

We Are Friends Because

we always work together as a team.

We Are Friends Because

no matter what the experience, it is more fun
when we share it.

We Are Friends Because . . .

you don't mind my tears.

we can tell each other the truth without sugarcoating it.

you help me sort through a problem
when I've made a mess of things.

you don't mind taking my phone call
in the middle of the night.

We Are Friends Because

we always share in each other's challenges
and celebrations.

We Are Friends Because

you have helped me reach a better
understanding of myself.

We Are Friends Because . . .

once I got to know you, I genuinely wanted
you to be a part of my life.

we share a similar vision and faith.

you never believe I ask too much of you.

you know when to give advice
and when to let me figure things out myself.

We Are Friends Because,

like me, you show your affection
for those you love.

We Are Friends Because

you never tire of playing Twister.

We Are Friends Because . . .

you always have a hug waiting for me.

you push me to make the right decisions.

our disagreements never threaten
our feelings for each other.

we do not covet what the other has
but share what we have instead.

We Are Friends Because

you always seem to understand
what I'm going through.

We Are Friends Because

you have always kept your promises to me.

We Are Friends Because

you always seem to know how to get me
in a better mood.

We Are Friends Because

although our lives have changed,
we haven't grown apart.

We Are Friends Because

you have never betrayed me.

We Are Friends Because

we play well together, and it doesn't matter who wins.

We Are Friends Because . . .

you are always quick to accept my apology,
and even quicker to give one.

you manage to keep me from getting into serious trouble.

you are not jealous of my other friends
and acquaintances.

you inspire me to do my best in everything.

We Are Friends Because

you can see things in me that others
have failed to see.

We Are Friends Because

we take turns being in charge.

We Are Friends Because

we always cover each other's back.

We Are Friends Because

we miss each other when we are apart.

We Are Friends Because . . .

I love you, and you love me, too.

you rescued me when I could not save myself.

time and distance do not change the way
we feel about each other.

you understand me well enough to know
what to take seriously and what to ignore.

We Are Friends Because

you have never told anyone about my
secret hiding place.

We Are Friends Because

you help me stay in a healthy state of mind.

We Are Friends Because

no matter how recently we last saw each other,
you are always glad to see me.

We Are Friends Because . . .

we have really, *really* gotten to know all the good, bad, and ugly stuff about each other.

you have never tried to make me be something I am not.

you can anticipate my mood just from the look on my face.

from you I derive strength and comfort.

We Are Friends Because

we give to each other before we take, and we
never take more than we give.

We Are Friends Because

you take care not to embarrass me, yet you keep me
from taking myself too seriously.

We Are Friends Because . . .

you always bring something back for me
when you go somewhere cool.

you always return what you have borrowed from me.

we can have fun doing almost anything, and . . .

we can have fun hanging out doing nothing.

We Are Friends Because

we are always there for each other, no matter
what the circumstances.

We Are Friends Because

we can laugh and scream together
without feeling foolish.

We Are Friends Because

you wouldn't think of celebrating something special
without having me there to celebrate too.

We Are Friends Because . . .

you know how to lighten my heart
when life weighs me down.

we still get along even when we don't see eye to eye.

we have a long and meaningful history together.

you don't minimize the things that are important to me.

We Are Friends Because

we can be our true selves around one another.

We Are Friends Because

you always know how to make
the best of a rainy day.

We Are Friends Because

you have made sure I was never left behind.

We Are Friends Because

you have never taken advantage of me.

We Are Friends Because

you know me better than anyone else does.

We Are Friends Because

we don't find it necessary to impress each other.

We Are Friends Because . . .

you don't mind going to extremes
to put a smile on my face.

you always tell me what I need to know,
even if I don't want to hear it.

you have never tried to make me feel
guilty about anything.

your encouragement helps me believe in myself.

We Are Friends Because

we both like chocolate sauce on our
pistachio ice cream.

We Are Friends Because

we won't let each other get away with something
we shouldn't get away with.

We Are Friends Because

we always share equally in the work,
the credit, and the rewards.

We Are Friends Because . . .

you help me without making me feel like
I owe you something in return.

even anger and disappointment doesn't wedge between us.

we pull together when the work is more
than only one can do.

we both know it was more than just dumb luck
that brought us together.

We Are Friends Because

you have proven to me more than once what
"You can count on me" means.

We Are Friends Because

we take care not to hurt each other
when we butt heads.

We Are Friends Because

you share my love for adventure.

We Are Friends Because . . .

you have never tried to make yourself
look better at my expense.

you look out for my safety and best interest.

you don't mind getting your hands dirty to help me.

you didn't stop caring about me when I
wasn't very nice to you.

We Are Friends Because

you motivate me when I'm having trouble taking
the next important step.

We Are Friends Because . . .

you've never told anyone about
that little thing I once told you about.

you don't use my nickname in public. Well, not too often.

you have contributed to my life in more ways
than I can count.

our similarities far outweigh our differences.

We Are Friends Because

we are comfortable seeing each other
at our worst.

We Are Friends Because

we compete for the fun, not the glory.

We Are Friends Because . . .

you never seem to tire of listening to me,
even if you have heard it all before.

you give me tough love when I need it.

you have never made me feel like you were waiting for someone better to come along.

you forgave me for that time when . . . well, you know.

We Are Friends Because

it is easy, and safe, to pour my heart out to you.

We Are Friends Because

you are always there to pick me up when I fall down.

We Are Friends Because . . .

you have never forgotten my birthday.

you never have so much to do that you can't stop
and have a little fun with me.

you remember our secret handshake.

you have taken up for me when others wouldn't.

We Are Friends Because

judgment has not clouded our acceptance
of each other.

We Are Friends Because

both our lives are enriched by our friendship.

ACKNOWLEDGMENTS

Once more I owe a heartfelt thanks to Ron Pitkin, my friend and publisher, who continues to have faith in the things I wish to write about, and the staff at Cumberland House, most notably my editor, Lisa Taylor, also a friend and trusted resource. Finally, I thank my wonderful wife, Jill, for her unwavering support and belief in me and for being my best friend of all time.

TO CONTACT THE AUTHOR

write in care of the publisher:
Cumberland House Publishing
431 Harding Industrial Drive
Nashville, TN 37211

or e-mail the author:
greg.lang@mindspring.com

visit the author's Web site:
gregoryelang.com